DANCING ON THE BRINK

ADAM HOLBROOK

authorHOUSE®

AuthorHouse™
1663 Liberty Drive
Bloomington, IN 47403
www.authorhouse.com
Phone: 1 (800) 839-8640

Published by AuthorHouse 02/05/2016

ISBN: 978-1-5049-7403-5 (sc)
ISBN: 978-1-5049-7402-8 (e)

Library of Congress Control Number: 2016900849

Print information available on the last page.

Preface

In the frosty February of 1978, during the first of my many hospitalizations at the Department of Veterans Affairs treatment facility in Marion, Indiana, I met and became instant friends with a very special nurse aide.

During one of our frequent chats she said something to me which I shall never fail to remember.

She said, "Adam, there is a part of you that is so logical, but there's another part of you that is so *crazy!!*"

Realistically looking back over the forty plus years that I have suffered from schizophrenia, I can without reservation state that pronouncement is an accurate appraisal of my psychological composition. I am indeed mentally untamed, but at all times I find myself dancing on the brink of reality - and hoping to fall in.

Be reminded as you read the following pages that the head of a person afflicted with schizophrenia is a very noisy place. Our thoughts are elusive as they dash willy-nilly through our consciousness and every moment seems to carry with it a new adventure in perplexity.

As you read this journey into the intriguing world of one man's mental illness, also remember that the events and people depicted are real.

Also bear in mind the medications written about in this account of my experiences have not generally been in use for several decades. Nowadays we have much more effective medicines with very few, if any, side affects. Therefore, people who suffer from any form of mental illness today have nothing to fear from modern medical science.

Lima, Ohio

July 30, 2014

I

The winter
1975 – 1976

In March of 1975 I was married in Middlesboro, Kentucky (for reasons which I would rather not discuss) to a girl who was fourteen years of age. As much as we were able, me with schizophrenia and Cindy being in her youth, we loved one another. However, we were both children, psychologically speaking, and were not at all prepared to function in the adult world in which we had suddenly found ourselves.

For the first few months of our marriage Cindy and I led a quiet, reserved life in which nothing memorable happened. Cindy continued her education and we were quite contented with one another. We attended church regularly and although our income was meager we were able to pay the rent on our single bedroom apartment and to provide for ourselves the necessities of life.

Then in early July of 1975 we became acquainted with a group of handicapped traveling sales people and were persuaded to throw in our lot with them. Cindy and I proved ourselves to be fairly competent sales representatives and didn't mind living out of suitcases. We loved traveling and passing through places we had never before seen. But when the manager of the troop discovered that my wife was only fourteen years of age we were both unceremoniously fired and sent home.

That was the beginning of our woes. Once back in our hometown of Lima, Ohio, Cindy and I found ourselves to be restless and moody. For the next few months we bounced from pillar to post, from village to city, until the December of 1975. We then took up residence in a very small mobile home in the same area of Shawnee Township, Ohio in which Cindy had been raised. Her old school friends, all of whom were younger than seventeen years of age, dropped in often and kept us entertained. Our home became a hang out where there was much underage drinking and drug related activity. It didn't dawn on me until years later that all of this could have placed me in serious trouble with the local law enforcement authorities.

About that time I came to possess something which nowadays has become indispensable – a credit card. I used it to buy things – ***many* t**hings. With cash advances I bought a small motorcycle and, in order to keep my balance, rode it with both feet gliding on the packed snow of the frozen winter streets. That winter was especially cold and my hands got chilled when I was riding the motorcycle so I bought a $60.00 pair of snowmobile gloves. Every time I was short of cash, I'd drive up to the ATM and get a cash advance, sometimes of more than $50.00. Well, all of this shortly caught up with me. I found myself deeply in debt and my Bankamericard canceled.

Not long after the first of 1976, Cindy was found to be with child. I was elated that I was going to be a father even though I had no idea of what parenting was all about. (After three more babies, I am still not certain that I have mastered the art.) Cindy realized that she was not ready to be a mother and became very resentful of me. We began to have violent verbal altercations and her friends would sometimes have to intervene before these arguments turned physical.

One evening Cindy and I were home alone and became involved in a noisy confrontation. She slapped my face so hard that I fell backward onto the sofa. She then jumped on top of me and proceeded to choke me. I didn't resist but after about thirty seconds she let go of me and tearfully apologized. We had a long talk that evening and that was the last heated exchange of words we had for the remainder of our time together.

The Spring
1976

The winter passed and sometime in March I came to the realization that if I was going to be a father I should show some responsibility and earnestly seek employment. Without much real effort I landed a job with the local franchise of a nationwide commercial moving and storage company. It was hard work, but I was proud of myself to have a job for I was raised in a family which had a very strong work ethic. At that time I was finding myself to be keenly identified with Merle Haggard's country music classic, "Working Man's Blues."

I decided then that I was not about to be on welfare (again) and that I would be a working man, thus following in the footsteps of both my step-father and my natural father. I took great satisfaction in being just a common laborer who being was paid an honest dollar and made me at least appear to myself as being a "man among men."

One day, two or so weeks after my being hired, there was not much going on in my workplace so my supervisor assigned to me the task of sweeping the warehouse, which was an especially menial pursuit. I told myself that I was a working man and sometimes working men had to take on chores which some would regard as being beneath their dignity.

While I was sweeping the (to say the least) spacious warehouse, I came to ponder some episodes of a very popular television series at that time, "Movin' On" which portrayed the life of two gypsy truckers played by actors Claude Akins and another man whose name now escapes me. In the mid to late seventies truck drivers had come to be regarded as folk heroes and citizen's band radios were the craze.

Suddenly I saw myself as being a television producer with a new twist on programs which featured tough, ruggedly independent truckers. Why not develop a television series which would be a spoof of the rough trucker's programs.

I began to fantasize about myself and actor David Cassidy being the stars of a comedy show featuring two fellows in the trucking business that were less than the typical super-masculine, testosterone laden drivers. "Sure," I began to tell myself, "That would be a hit!" The longer I thought about that idea the funnier (in my own mind) it became. I even began to plan episodes of this television production to the point of being carried away by the power of the rapidly developing notion.

I went on sweeping, becoming more and more amused with myself and getting to the point of being almost giddy. At that moment I looked around and found myself to have an audience of puzzled-looking co-workers. My boss was among them and interrupted my musings by shouting, "Adam! Let's go have lunch."

We made our way to a nearby tavern. As we were sipping cold beer my boss informed me that my services were no longer needed in his moving and storage company. He advised me that I needed to seek some sort of job training. He was also quite adamant in stating that I would just simply never find any success in the trucking business.

I was devastated.

In that hour or so of sweeping the warehouse, the die had been cast. The cornerstone of my lunacy which was to develop during the following summer had been put in place. I was well on my way to being swept under by the force of a full blown psychotic break down.

Immediately after the "lunch break" I returned home and when I walked through the door, Cindy looked at me quizzically and said, "I thought you were at work!"

"I was." I replied and then added, "I got fired."

Cindy sat down at our dining table, buried her face in her hands and began to sob.

"Honey….." I said putting my arm around her shoulders in an effort to comfort her.

"Go away!" she shouted. "Just go away!"

Seeing there was no way to console her, I left Cindy and went to a nearby diner and ordered a cup of coffee. I began to at least try to find an idea – any idea - of what to do and which direction to go. It came to me, from out of nowhere, that the home office of the moving company (from which I had just been dismissed) had a program called the "summer fleet" in which college students could find work for the summer. This, I found out later, with dismay, this was not a fact, but a false idea. But I resolved to go the headquarters of the moving company in Ft. Wayne, Indiana and sign up for the "summer fleet." I was thinking that even temporary work was better than none at all.

Early the next morning, while Cindy was still sleeping, I left for Indiana. But I was delusional and not thinking appropriately. It simply never dawned on me I didn't have enough gasoline to get home and virtually no cash with which to buy any.

After a few wrong turns and asking for directions several times, I found my way to the home office. There I was not so gently informed there was no such thing as a "summer fleet." With tears stinging my cheeks I returned to my automobile and sat there for a good long while.

It then came to me that my sister, Rhonda, lived in eastern Indiana near a small town called Milford. I felt in some way refreshed and becoming more brain sick by the moment as I set out for Milford. When I arrived there I inquired as to where Rhonda and Glenn (last name must remain unstated) lived. By sheer good fortune I found a man who was acquainted with them and gave me directions to their house.

The house where Rhonda and Glenn lived was a small home in the center of a run down mobile home park adjacent to a small lake. I had intended to borrow money in order to get home but when Rhonda came to the door she threw it open wide and lovingly embraced me. She served coffee and we talked for nearly an hour. I was about to ask for the loan when she wanted to know what I was doing in Indiana. As I explained she listened and then asked me if I knew how to weld. Of course I knew how to weld. Our step-father had been a welder for many years and had taught me the art when I was yet a boy. She informed that the small factory where Glenn was employed expanding and needed five welders. She assured me Glenn could get me hired.

I called Cindy to tell her where I was and what I was doing. She was furious but I talked her down and assured her that if I got the job I would come to get her as soon as I drew my first pay check.

Presently Glenn came home and to make a long story short I was hired as a welder the next day. My job was welding together mobile home frames. Although it was a rather menial occupation, I loved it. I was a *real* man who was doing a *real* man's job.

Glenn and Rhonda had enthusiastically agreed they would allow Cindy and I to board with them until we got on our feet. That was a decision of theirs for which I will remain eternally grateful.

I worked my first two weeks and with pay check in hand I discussed with Glenn how best to go back to Ohio and retrieve my very pregnant young wife and our belongings. Glenn owned a pick up truck and we enlisted the help of another couple who also owned a truck. We were off to Ohio that evening. The couple who accompanied us to Ohio were quiet, but pleasant people who didn't seem to mind helping out.

Early the next morning when we arrived at our Ohio destination we were all tired because we had been awake all night so Cindy and I lent our bed to the quiet couple so they could rest. I don't recall if it was me or Glenn who bought them but we had a box of pastries on hand to eat for breakfast as we packed.

Again my memory fails me, but for some reason I had to leave the house to buy a thing that we needed (perhaps it was a roll of packing tape) but in order to get there I had to cross over Interstate Highway 75. There I spotted a man who was about fifty years of age, in soiled and tattered clothing, who was hitch-hiking. My heart went out to the man and when I invited him back to my house for coffee and doughnuts he seemed to be quite appreciative.

When I showed up at home with the vagabond, Glenn was incensed. He seized his rifle out of his truck, aimed it toward the poor man and ordered him off the premises. As Rhonda subdued Glenn I went inside and returned with a doughnut and gave it to the man, who ate it hungrily. After a further tirade from Glenn I got the man once more into my car and drove him back to the highway. When I returned Rhonda said aptly, "You treated that bum better then the people who were here helping you out." As she turned her back I realized that my heart had been in the right place – and the wrong place – at the same time.

That spring of 1976 I settled into my job. Glenn and I worked every day and after work dropped into a neighborhood watering hole in North Webster for a beer or two. When we got home, as Rhonda and Cindy prepared dinner, Glenn and I went fishing at one of the two small lakes which were nearby. I wasn't much of a fisherman (I am still not) but Glenn taught me what he could about catching fish. Within a few weeks Cindy and I began to seriously seek a place of our own. This is when my life began to go totally bizarre.

The Summer 1976

Cindy and I moved into a house just to the east of Syracuse, Indiana which was not far from the shop where I worked. The home was constructed in the early fifties and was quite modern in its day. The exterior was made up of painted concrete blocks and the living room had walls of knotty pine. From the moment I set foot in that house I became aware of a very peculiar feeling that I had been there before. This was not simply a case of déjà vu. It was a much more pronounced feeling. I felt as though I **belonged there**. It seemed as though I was **home**. But I sensed something which I found to be inexplicably unsettling about the place. I had morose impressions which are every bit as convoluted to me now as they were then. But then, the life of a schizophrenic is made up of complex thought patterns and fleeting, intangible impressions so I passed off these initial apprehensive feelings as "just my illness." Still, I sensed a spirit about the place which was oppressively evil, as if some ghastly event had taken place there.

After a about a month of working as a welder I was reassigned to the job of being a "utility man," which is a person who performs odd jobs around the factory and could be asked to perform a number of chores. For a period of a few weeks I worked at assembling the components necessary to build a certain type of mobile home frame. It was very repetitive and maddeningly monotonous work.

My fertile mind ran almost unrestrained while assembling those parts and I began to entertain some very peculiar thoughts, which to me at that time seemed quite ordinary and unquestionably plausible. That is one of the main deceptions of schizophrenia. Downright weird ideation seems to be well within the sphere of the believability. The suffering person's mind lies to itself.

As I toiled I began to hallucinate. I was "hearing" The Doobie Brothers' recording of the song "White Sun." (The song mentioned is a piece of music is on the "Toulouse Street" album.) As I pondered the lyrics I was convinced that this particular song was being sent to me telepathically as a message from the angels. The "White Sun" in the song was the only light source for a civilization of miniature, subterranean people. It was not unlike the experience of the main character of the classic novel **Gulliver's Travels**. I was the only normal sized person who dwelt in the cavern and had to be very cautious so as not to tread upon these small people, whom I believed to be the descendants of Gulliver's Lilliputians. But by being on the surface of the earth I had shirked my responsibility to keep the white sun shining by replacing, when it burned out, the white incandescent light bulb on the ceiling of the grotto. I was the keeper of the "White Sun" and it was the mission of my life to find the way back to the little people who were depending upon me to provide their only source of illumination. I was overcome with panic when I thought of the bulb already being burned out and those helpless, diminutive humans were wandering about their cavern in total darkness.

It was about this time that Cindy's cousin Brenda came from Ohio to visit. On her arrival I immediately came to be persuaded that Brenda was not a cousin at all but the sister of young actress Melissa Gilbert (of Little House on the Prairie fame) to whom Brenda does bear a genuine resemblance. A day or so after her arrival I asked Brenda if she was, in fact the sister of Miss Gilbert. Cindy's cousin appeared bewildered as she denied any relationship. Brenda became "weirded out" by her cousin's husband and requested to be driven home after just a few days.

Time went by and after three weeks of hallucinating and suffering profound remorse for abandoning my responsibilities to the teeny cave dwellers, I was ready for a break. I was sent to work in the paint shed, taking the place of a young fellow who had been caught masturbating while on the job and relieved of his duties.

The paint shed was everything its name implied. The finished frames were stacked six high on a movable platform and it was my job to climb among the frames and spray every square inch of them with a coating of glossy black paint. It was the dirtiest, most strenuous and most thankless job the shop had to offer. I returned home from work every evening with streaks of black paint covering a good portion of my body. I hated this job. I was again a working man who had been required to perform a quite unglamorous (and hazardous) task.

Apparently my work was not satisfactory and I was permanently assigned to duties outside of the industrial unit which had provided me with employment. I was fired.

Time is not easy to keep track of when one is, beyond any doubt, brain sick but I knew I was fired off my job in mid June.

While working at the mobile home frame factory, I became acquainted with a co-worker who, along with his wife, was the proprietors of a small pizza business. Cindy and I became regular customers. One day, over lunch at the factory, we were conversing and I mentioned that we had moved into a house just across the road from the western shore of Lake Wawasee. He said that he knew the house and that he and his wife had considered renting it but couldn't afford the monthly lease payments. (Neither could Cindy and I, but that is another story.) He then said something that was most peculiar. He stated, "I thought those walls were dynamite."

In mid 1970's terminology, to call something "dynamite" meant that it was beautiful, outstanding, or in some way superb. Immediately my degenerate mind went to work.

Because he described the knotty pine walls as being "dynamite" it meant (to me at least) that there were dynamite charges planted within the walls of the house when it was constructed. Anyone inside would be shredded to smithereens if a malevolent person with a transmitter operating on a certain radio frequency could detonate them.

This series of perfectly insane thought patterns did indeed detonate something - they set off a veritable poop storm within my mind.

I really have no idea of how to proceed from this point, but I must press on. Here goes......

If you have read my first book, **Dear Mom**, you will know that I had believed my natural father, Gale Holbrook and my step father, Robert Aab to have been among the personal, Secret Service bodyguards of none other than President John F. Kennedy. This belief emerged from the pits of my depraved psyche in the summer of 1976 and remained on into the years of 1977-1978 when the happenings described in Dear **Mom** took place. Going further into the depths of my madness, I believed (as also described also in **Dear Mom)** JFK to be my biological father instead of Gale Holbrook.

The idea suddenly captivated me that the house Cindy and I had moved into was, in the past, a hideaway for organized crime figures. I was fully persuaded that JFK, Robert Aab (my stepfather) and Gale Holbrook (my biological father) were deeply involved. In the kitchen ceiling was a passage which allowed access to the attic. To my way of thinking this passage led to an escape hatch which I sought for several weeks to find, but failed. I now know that I didn't locate it because it simply didn't exist.

In the garage I found a collection of fluorescent letters, such as one would use on a mail box to indicate who owned the box and thus dwelt in the house. I studied these letters and found they could be used to spell a name – Ada Zeldinger.

"Aha!" The outrageous idea which struck me could almost be classified as a distorted epiphany. "So *that's* what happened in this house!! A woman named Ada Zeldinger was murdered here!! I live in a haunted house!!

As I pondered the demise of the fictitious lady, Ada Zeldinger, I thought I should consult someone who might have known the full story.

My nearest neighbors lived in a small house which was located about fifty yards to the north at the end of a gravel lane. As I approached I could discern that my neighbors, who were seated in lawn chairs in back of the house were not pleased with the idea of entertaining visitors. I made myself at home and planted my posterior in the only unoccupied lawn chair. The people were obviously annoyed, but annoyed people had never hindered me before. I began to interrogate my neighbors, as if I were an investigating police officer, as to circumstances which surrounded the death of one Ada Zeldinger.

As the lady of the house went inside to phone the police, her husband not so politely ordered me off the premises. Greatly dismayed, I left.

I would say it was about twenty minutes later that two deputies from the Kosiosko county sheriff's department were knocking at my back door. They advised me to stay away from the neighbor's house or be arrested. I told the deputies their advice was well taken and I wouldn't bother anyone from then on. I watched, with much relief, out the front window as the lawmen drove away.

The only comment from Cindy was "I wish they had taken you with them."

That night was, for me, a sleepless one. For the time being I had forgotten about Ada Zeldinger and began to think in other directions. Across the road from our home was beautiful, pristine, Lake Wawasee. I began to believe that as year old child I had been held in JFK's arms on the lawn of the house and while pointing to the water and said, "Wa!! Wa!! See?" Therefore the lake had been named Lake Wawasee according to what I had requested. Being convinced I had picked out a name for a body of water was the least of my atypical psychological exploits. As the summer wore on they became progressively more extreme.

On the day before Cindy's trip to the hospital in Warsaw, (which will be explained below) I was, at the crack of dawn, across the driveway from our house. There was a small garden in which a number of flat limestone rocks were lying. I had been awake for at least thirty hours and was quite energetically turning over those rocks as if I were expecting to find something under one of them. Cindy came out of the house, walked into the garden, and asked me what I was doing. "Looking for Paul McCartney!" I replied, being fully convinced that if I overturned the right rock, Paul McCartney would crawl out from under it. Cindy just looked at me in bewilderment, returned to the house, and went back to bed.

A few days before this event, Cindy and I were having dinner at a fast food restaurant in Syracuse when I observed a handsome young couple seated not far from us. They had the mannerisms and regal bearing of two young people who had been reared in a quite wealthy family. Immediately my warped psyche went to work. They were Caroline Kennedy and John Jr. who had come to get a close up look of their elder half brother! *Of course!*

Please recognize that my recollections of that summer are nebulous, indistinct and very difficult to write with some degree of order. Many any other things may have taken place, but I will only recount events of which I am sure.

Toward the latter part of June (I think) Cindy was hospitalized for what was called "premature labor," probably brought on by the inconceivable stress my behavior had triggered in her. The doctor in charge of her case was quite indignant as he informed me that Cindy's condition had improved but he was nonetheless keeping her overnight for observation. He then stated that he would see what he could do about getting me "locked up" for having sexual contact with and impregnating such a young girl. He considered this to be criminal even though we were (at least under Kentucky law) quite married.

That afternoon, after Cindy had refused to see me, I drove the thirty five miles from the hospital in Warsaw (Indiana) to our house. (I call it a house, not a home.

There is a difference.) All the way I closely observed my automobile's fuel gauge. I was unsure if I would have enough gasoline to get back to Syracuse, let alone return to Warsaw the next day.

As the sun was setting that evening I suddenly realized that I was alone. Not just simply alone at home, but alone in the world. Cindy hated me. My family hated me. My former coworkers (in Ohio and Indiana) had hated me. I had left behind every friend I thought I had and they all hated me... It seemed as though even our two dogs hated me. I felt that God hated me. Worst of all, I hated myself.

All of this was much too psychologically excruciating to contemplate. I had to escape and I did so by becoming totally and unreservedly out of my mind. It wasn't an entirely conscious decision. The need to escape was far too compelling. I simply couldn't offer any resistance and succumbed to the all out assault I had launched against my own sense of reason.

I am uncertain about much of what transpired that night. I do know that I had my stereo blasting out music throughout those hours. I had a good collection of eight track tapes and I know I played every one at least twice.

One moment I found myself laughing hysterically and in the next I was weeping uncontrollably. Just as the sun became visible above the horizon at the end of that long night I joyfully contemplated Barry Manilow's song, "Daybreak" which was being played at full volume on my stereo. I stood at my front door singing along with Barry as loudly as possible and beheld the sunrise through the small window of the door. I was suddenly besieged by a feeling of unmitigated joy which was so intense it was without a doubt the product of a sick mind.

My countenance fell as I saw two antique fire trucks drive past the house. Fire, so I was persuaded by my delusions, was the symbol of love. Two fire trucks on the way to Syracuse meant they were on a mission to extinguish the love (fire) the people there felt for me. My grief was ended in a split second.

"Don't be sad Adam! It's daybreak!!" I shouted.

"It's *Daybreak*!!"

I was suddenly unconfined by the dismal psychological drama in which I had, for the sake of survival, play-acted for most of my life.

"It's Daybreak!!"

The magnificent sun was rising and with it came the expulsion of the cold shadows in which I had been blindly stumbling. The night was over!! It was *daybreak!!* I was supreme, ecstatic and quite invincible!!

I then came upon a grand (or so I thought) idea. I looked on the label of one of my Barry Manilow recordings, scribbled the record company's mailing address on a scrap of paper, and then got on the telephone. I called the information operator and obtained the telephone number of the music publisher. I then called Western Union and sent Mr. Manilow a telegram in the care of his record company. I don't recall the text, but be assured the message did not contain anything intelligible. All I know is that it was, to understate myself, idiotic. Of *course* Barry would respond! I had written his songs.

About a week later Mr. Manilow returned my message. Rhonda happened to be at my place and took the call. She says she had a difficult time explaining to a famous entertainer why her little brother would send to him such an off the wall correspondence. She was without doubt mortified.

The Return to Reality?

The time was nearly noon when my telephone rang. It was a nurse from the hospital on the line who informed me that Cindy was being released and I should come and pick her up. My jubilation of the earlier morning hours had abated somewhat and I was just barely under more control of my mental processes than I had been in the preceding hours.

With seemingly hundreds of disjointed thoughts cascading through my mind, I locked both of our dogs in the garage and set out toward Warsaw, heading south on Indiana Route 13. I can't recall anything about the excursion until I had turned Westbound on US Route 30. After perhaps three or four miles, my automobile engine suddenly stopped running. I was able to guide the vehicle to a space nearly off the roadway and tried in vain to restart the engine, but to no avail. I sat there along the side of the busy thoroughfare in amazed confusion and could not come up with a reason why an automobile engine would just turn itself off. (The thought that I could have been out of gasoline didn't dawn on me.)

I didn't know what else to do other than set off on foot and after an undetermined distance and passage of time, I wandered onto the crowded parking lot of shopping center. There appeared to be a sort of carnival going on, so I just amused myself by watching the little children enjoying themselves on the kiddie rides.

Suddenly I was startled back to reality and remembered the reason for my trip to Warsaw. I had come to pick up Cindy at the hospital! With no thought as to the consequences of my actions and with slightly less than two dollars in my pocket, I telephoned a taxi service and instructed them to send a driver to get Cindy at the hospital and then pick up me at the shopping center. I called Cindy at the hospital and told her to expect the taxi and to wait in the lobby.

Then I waited......and waited......and waited. After nearly three hours of expecting to have a ride back to Syracuse, and with no clue as to Cindy's whereabouts, I gave up and went walking eastbound on US 30. I was able to hitch a ride with a kind soul as far as Route 13 and then, on foot, proceeded north.

I was hot, tired, hungry, thirsty and perspiring but I trudged on. After an hour or so of being a bedraggled pedestrian, I decided to take a rest break and seated myself in the grass along the side of the road – and bawled. I wanted more than anything to do away with myself. Not even my affection for Cindy, or the love I felt for our as yet unborn child could be balanced against the total hopelessness within my soul.

Sobbing, I popped one lens out of the frame of my eyeglasses and attempted to slash myself. The edge wasn't sharp enough so I stomped on the lens with the heel of my right boot and attempted to shatter it in an effort to create a sharp edge which I could use to puncture my skin. I, all of a sudden, realized the lens was plastic and couldn't easily be smashed. I then spied a broken soda bottle. I seized it and put the sliver of glass to my left wrist. There was still no break in my skin. I was furious and jammed the point into my flesh and twisted it again, and again. Still no wound appeared.

Greatly dismayed, I cast aside the glass fragment and sobbed. I couldn't even succeed in killing myself. All I had accomplished was to ruin my glasses. I was a total loser.

A Tale of Three Hospitals

When I had regained my composure I was able to obtain a ride all the way to Syracuse. When I entered the back door of our house Cindy was furious and made that fact known to me in no uncertain terms. She told me of the unpleasant exchange of words between herself and the taxi driver when she explained that she had no money. Cindy was forced to turn over several pieces of her jewelry to the driver and was not at all happy about it. The cabby told Cindy the jewelry was not nearly enough to pay the fare and that he would contact the law enforcement authorities as soon as he got back to Warsaw.

I recalled the day before, prior to taking Cindy to the hospital, I had visited Rhonda and while at her home had launched into a rather lengthy report concerning all of the stars of the recording business I had written for and/or produced. This seemed to alarm my sister and I feared that she and Glenn would force me into a hospital.

It was nearly nightfall and having been awake for many hours I was exhausted. I locked all of the doors in the house and harshly ordered Cindy not to allow anyone to enter, especially Glenn and Rhonda. Half expecting Cindy and I to be arrested at any time, I laid myself down on the sofa and immediately dropped off to sleep.

I wasn't asleep for long when I was awakened with a start to the sound of someone rapping with insistence at my back door. The voices I heard from outside were familiar. They belonged to Rhonda and Glenn.

"Don't open that door!" I barked at Cindy.

She sent an icy stare my way for a few seconds then unlocked the door and allowed Glenn and Rhonda into the house. Along with them was another couple. The man I knew well, (He was a former co-worker), but I had never seen the lady. I presumed she was his spouse.

I was physically persuaded to get into one of the automobiles outside. Cindy and I rode in the back seat other couple's rattle trap Chevrolet station wagon while Rhonda and Glenn took the lead in their pick up truck. I repeatedly asked where we were going, but was not-so- gently ordered to keep quiet. Cindy sat next to me with tears welled up in her eyes.

Before we had gone many miles I realized that I had been kidnapped and was being transported to a hospital in Ft. Wayne. I knew that to resist would have been pointless, so I accepted my circumstances and deep within me knew that a hospital was probably the safest place for me to be at that time. After all, I was the eldest Kennedy grandchild and there were people at large who would seek to do me harm. To go was in my best interests. I needed to be confined and out of sight.

The old Chevrolet in which we were riding was quite a sophisticated masquerade – the auto glass was bullet proof and there were firearms concealed within the vehicle. For the first time in many days I thought myself to be in safe hands. I knew I was being transported in an armor plated vehicle to a secure destination. I sensed I could trust the people who were taking me on this jaunt to whatever location in Ft.Wayne, Indiana. These were people who sincerely loved me! At long last I was to fulfill my destiny!

I was relaxed and was enjoying myself as we arrived at Parkview Hospital in Ft. Wayne. Rhonda and Glenn went inside and some time later emerged from the building. I sat in the back seat of the old station wagon smiling as Cindy, seated next to me, wiping her eyes which were red and puffy from the shedding of tears.

Glenn and our other escort conversed at length and then we were off to another hospital because Parkview refused to admit me due to my lack of health insurance.

We departed Parkview and before long we arrived at St. Joseph Hospital where I was again refused treatment. There was only one more place in Ft.Wayne where I might be cared for, which was Lutheran Hospital. We went there and I was admitted very late in the evening, probably past midnight.

Often, after reading my first three books, people ask me how I recall so many events related to my illness with such a great degree of coherence and clarity. It isn't effortless and it is a fill-in-the-blank process. Often my recollections are disjointed and imprecise. It takes much thought and many hours of reflection, which is precisely why I am not as prolific a writer as I'd like to be. Often my reflections resemble what can to be compared to bad dreams – hazy and ethereal – surreal, but none the less substantial. But I digress.

My reasons in stating the above have to do with entering an uncharted mental realm, into which I have been most reluctant to delve. I liken it to a psychological mine field. Any of these memories could blow up in my face and precipitate a relapse into the wild world of schizophrenia, but I am willing to take that risk. This is because it may provide insight into why I was the way I was and possibly some clues as to why I think as I do now. I pray this excursion into the murky depths of one person's madness will also be of help and comfort to you, the readers, also. Are you ready? Let's get back to the narrative.

The next few hours were indistinct, not unlike looking at events and surroundings through a thick sheet of smoked glass. I have no recollection of my in-processing at the hospital at all, other than being elated by a sense of security which had taken me captive. I was expectant and energized as though something truly momentous was about to happen.

"It's *daybreak*!" I screamed to myself. "It's *daybreak*!"

When I came to myself, perhaps several hours later, I was bedded down in a very small room, alone with my blossoming psychosis. A florescent light was faintly illuminating the area above and slightly behind my head, was scarcely driving shadows from the room. I looked to my left and on the night stand found my eyeglasses and placed them on my face. I removed them in disgust because I couldn't see a thing through them although they had been repaired by a kind hearted soul there on the unit. The plastic lenses had been too badly scratched. On the bed to my right I found a device which, I supposed, was for me to summon the hospital staff if I needed any type of assistance.

I fingered the appliance long enough to discover that it had a second function. It also contained a radio, which I switched on and tuned in radio station WOWO. I had listened to WOWO since I was young and had always enjoyed the top 40 hits format of the station.

It was at this time my psychosis kicked into high gear.

As the disk jockey played his line up of then popular tunes, I was beset by the belief that I had written each and every song.

When Abba's "Dancing Queen" came on the air I was persuaded that I had penned the song as a way of describing myself at one of my junior high school record hops. I found that both disturbing and embarrassing because I was of the opinion that a male who was thought of as being a "queen" referred to his possessing homosexual attributes. By and by a song by the duo Sonny and Cher came through the radio speaker. I heard my mother's voice whispering in both ears that I should be sunny and share – in other words be cheerful and generous. I made every effort to resist these notions but the energy behind them was profound and overpowering.

At that time television theme songs were at the top of the hit parade and I became convinced that I had not only penned the tunes, but produced the hit television programs they represented. I was ecstatic. "I really *am* a star!!" Thin Lizzie's "The Boys are Back In Town" was on the hit parade then and suggested to me that my friends would provide my revenge on those who had purposefully and systematically caused me psychological suffering.

Half realizing this was nonsense, I switched off the radio. As I tried in vain to go sleep I began to hallucinate. In my left ear, I heard my step father whispering "You want to be a *farmer*!" on my right I heard the voice of John F. Kennedy saying, "No. You want to be *president*!" Then my mother was shouting (in both ears) "I told you to be a *good* boy!" Another voice which seemingly came from everywhere was repeating itself saying "You wanna be a *truck driver*, don't' you?" I could also "hear" Paul McCartney (with his distinctly

British accent) saying, "Wouldn't you rather be a rock star like me?"

This went on for the better part of an hour until, in an effort to drown out the brutal onslaught of auditory hallucinations, I switched the radio back on.

The first thing I heard was The Silver Convention disco hit, "Get Up and Boogie!" So, I got up and boogied. I went skipping out of the room and down the semi-darkened hallway until I was confronted by a huge human being whose first name. I found out later, was Mark. He escorted me back to my assigned cubicle and not-so-gently suggested that I make an effort to sleep.

I unenthusiastically returned to bed and immediately became aware of the phantomlike voice of my mother speaking in both of my ears.

"You created this world!!' the otherworldly voice murmured, then followed up with a startlingly shrill command,

"Now you *live* in it Buddy!!"

I felt as though my body had lifted itself an inch off the bed and for the next eight or so minutes unrestrained horror gripped every fiber of my being. It required every ounce of courage and self restraint I could draw together to keep from running, in a screaming fit, down the corridor. In that span of time I believed that I was Jesus Christ, the heavenly individual who assisted God in the creation of the universe. I had the sins of all mankind on my shoulders. Out of the blue it dawned on me that I would have to commit suicide to redeem the people of the world. I have never, before or since been gripped by such panic as I was in those few moments. I struggled with the urge to get up and run, as if I could somehow escape the goings on in my own mind.

"I am *God!!* I gasped.

I *am God!!"*

My heart was throbbing, my body shook violently and I was profusely perspiring, but as swiftly as the episode of fright had come upon me, it was gone. Greatly relieved, I gathered from deep within me, what self-possession I could. The intense storm of euphoria returned to me and, if anything, was more pronounced than it had been just a few moments earlier.

I was then taken captive by the idea that I was bedded down in an upscale hospital and the presidential suite which former president Richard Nixon had often occupied was just across the hall. Through all of the psychological contortions I had failed to retain the information as to exactly where I was.

The voices and delusions of grandeur (song writing) continued throughout the remainder of the night. At daybreak I was still not in control of myself and singing, at the top of my lungs, to the tune of an old Charlie Pride song,

"Is anybody going to San Antone

or Phoenix Arizona?

Anyplace is all right as long as I

don't have go down to Richmond!"

At the time I didn't consciously know this, but in Richmond, Indiana there is a state psychiatric hospital and the staff had already discussed the possibility of my being transferred there. It was uncanny. I seemed to have knowledge of what the staff was contemplating.

After an hour or so of thoroughly butchering a good country song I sang myself into an uneasy sleep.

The Eighth Floor

I felt as though I had slept all of fifteen minutes when a red headed young nurse aide awakened me and inquired as to whether or not I'd like something to eat. As I opened my glassy eyes and stared with some confusion on the face of the girl, I nodded and sat up in the bed. The young lady drew the curtains open.

The morning sun nearly blinded me. I was squinting as I attempted compose myself. The events (and madness) of the preceding hours were foggy and vague, as if they were nothing more than bad dreams – *very* bad dreams. I shuddered as I thought of my few moments as "God "and wished *that* was also just a bad dream. The searing pain within my heart with which I had wrestled for months erupted in flood of uncontaminated anguish as I realized the events of the night before were not dreams. They were all too real. I was nearly at the point of tears but I swallowed hard and was barely able to maintain my self-possession.

The young girl interrupted my reverie and I struggled to focus my eyes.

"How you feeling?"

"Okay I guess." I managed to blurt out, and then asked, "What time is it?"

"It's time you got up. It's eight thirty. I heard you had a hell of a night."

"Oh, it was hell all right."

"You seem to be in better shape than you were. C'mon, I'll show you to your breakfast. I think you need to get out of this tiny room for a while. It's like being in a closet"

I slipped my posterior off the bed and my knees immediately buckled. I fell into the arms of the young staff woman. How she had the strength to hold me and retain her balance I haven't a clue how but, with much difficulty, she kept the both of us from hitting the floor.

I stepped out into the corridor on my unsteady legs, and asked the young damsel about our location. She explained that I had been admitted to the eight floor of Lutheran Hospital in Ft. Wayne, Indiana just after midnight and had kept nearly the whole unit awake until six a.m.

"Lutheran Hospital?!" I exclaimed. "This is Walter Reed! President Nixon's suite is across the hall from mine!" The girl looked with wide eyes into my face, but remained speechless.

I looked to my left and saw there was a short hallway with six other doors visible. To my right there were two doors and the nurse's station in view. We proceeded in the direction of the nurse's station and rounded a corner to the right at which time I beheld a very long corridor with a large and well lit area at the opposite end.

As we drew closer to the room I could discern the sounds of animated conversation and some laughter. When we reached the end of the hallway, I came into the company of the other patients on the unit. Some were jovial, some quietly sullen. As they turned to look on me, some smiled and others grunted in disapproval. I became very self-conscious and wolfed down my breakfast with little sense of etiquette, all the while studying the faces of my fellow patients.

On my way down the long corridor to get my morning repast I had taken note of the many doors which lined both sides of the way. But, at breakfast I hadn't noticed many persons who dined in the communal area.

Many of the other patients, I discerned, had chosen to dine in their rooms.

I remained convinced that I was the son of John F. Kennedy and that, when I was a child, he had visited me in the dead of night only to find me asleep. Then, I hit upon an idea which was surely bound to impress the Kennedy family. I intended to pace the long corridors of the unit to which I was restricted until I had covered the gap between Washington D.C. and my childhood home near the village of Westminster, Ohio. President Kennedy had come that distance to see me, so I would, symbolically at least, go the same distance to where he was.

My "journey" began in early afternoon and continued until just after 10 pm that evening when Mark (the psychiatric technician mentioned earlier) physically restrained and forcibly compelled me to go to my room. My verbal protests were to no avail and Mark told me the next step would be my going into lock-up. Since I found the prospects of being locked in a padded seclusion room to be unpleasant, I unenthusiastically (and silently) went to bed without any further resistance.

At some point during the night I had slipped out of bed and, with a bar of soap, wrote the words, "I love you

Ft. Wayne!" on the window pane behind the curtain. I wrote it backward, knowing that it would be legible to anyone who happened to be on the street looking up. I wanted my fans to know I was being held captive on the eighth floor of Lutheran Hospital. I falsely presumed they would to come to my rescue, storm the hospital and by force obtain my release. Then I would be revealed to the world in all my glory.

A Tale of Two Needles

Judging the passage of time accurately, without the benefit of a watch or calendar and especially when one is in the throes of a major psychotic episode, as I was, is next to impossible. An individual in that condition seems to live in a state of timelessness. The hours and minutes seem to drift over one another. The result is the brain sick person has no inkling of how much time has elapsed, even from one minute to the next. It is not unlike existing without any sense that time is fleeting by. This is an extremely complicated concept to elucidate, but having done my best, I will continue with my narrative.

If I recall correctly (it is doubtful that I have) on the first Sunday afternoon following my hospital admission I received my initial visitors. As I was enjoying a much needed period of rest, Rhonda and my mother burst into the cubicle, which was the only few square feet of Lutheran Hospital that I could claim. They were enraged and noisily expounding about how I had brought dishonor and disgrace upon the family. They harangued me about how ashamed there were to be my relatives and spoke many other equally unsavory words of contempt. (Having said that, I will inform the reader that over the years my family and I have mended fences and now are getting along well.)

Having been so abruptly awakened, I was also in a fighting mood and a shouting match immediately ensued.

In the midst of the chaos going on in the room, a nurse delicately rapped on the door and entered with a hypodermic syringe filled with some sort of white milky liquid. This nearly incited a physical altercation. The nurse rather sheepishly indicated she had some medication for me.

"You two barge in here and start a fight!! Then *she* shows up with a needle!! You had this all planned out didn't you?!"

I turned and angrily glared at the nurse.

"Your timing was *flawless*!!" I bellowed.

At that point Rhonda and Mom marched out of the room, leaving me to contend with just the middle aged nurse. I was aware that to resist would lead to further problems and so I grudgingly allowed the lady to thrust the needle into the left cheek of my bare buttocks. Looking rather relieved after she had administered the injection, she strained to give me an apologetic smile and left the room gently closing the door behind her.

I remained in an attitude of controlled rage as I violently turned on the bed to lie on my back, and jerked up my pajama bottom. Those actions sent streaks of shooting pain through the lower third of my back and left hip area. I was told years later the medicine which was administered that day is a very thick substance and injections of it can be quite painful. That information was *not* news to me.

After what seemed to be a span of fifteen or so minutes my body began to perform in a very peculiar way. The first unusual thing to happen was my mandible muscles became very tight and my jaw pulled painfully to the right. I began to drool and found myself unable to speak. At almost that same time, my left arm pulled itself tightly against my chest. Then my left ankle excruciatingly twisted itself into a position which caused my left foot to turn sideways. I was helpless to control the onset of these contortions and could not possibly have performed these feats while not under the influence of some sort of drug.

I was suffering unspeakable agony as I slipped off of the bed and with great difficulty hobbled my way toward the nurse's station. Before I had been "walking" ten feet, a staff member, looking up over the desk, saw me struggling to get down the corridor.

"Oh my God!" she gasped. 'Gwen! Get the doctor on the phone!"

I quizzically looked at the nurse who had ran to my side, seeming to ask,

"*What* is going on?!"

The lady informed me I was having a reaction to the medication and that she would help me back to my room and I would be more comfortable.

"*Comfortable?*" I thought to myself.

I was escorted back to my bed and lay in unmitigated misery while the doctor was called. It took some time to reach him, as he was otherwise occupied on the golf course. Over the telephone (from the country club) the doctor ordered the antidote, which had to come upstairs from the hospital pharmacy. All the while I was on my bed writhing and drooling in unadulterated torment.

At last the same nurse as before shot my behind (the right cheek this time) full of the antidote and then remained at my bedside to be sure that I was getting relief. Gradually my muscles began to loosen and the discomfort gradually subsided. I drew a deep breath and heaved a healthy sigh. Though my body remained sore, I was able, at last, to relax. The ordeal was over.

The People

There were fellow patients on the unit where I was confined who have left indelible impressions in my mind which will be with me until my dying day and possibly beyond. I remember James, the recovering cocaine addict who sported bulky eyeglasses and Carolyn, a pathetic young lady who would almost daily find a means of lacerating herself. There was also Jason, a tall chap with bushy red hair who had been caught in the act of sexually molesting his girlfriend's four year old daughter. Others too, were present whose faces are vivid in my memory, but their names have faded from my remembrance with the passage of time.

Two people whom I recall with genuine fondness were a young man, Chuck, who suffered with Bi-polar disorder (called Manic Depression at that time) and Sarah, a petite eleven year old whose diagnosis was never disclosed.

Chuck had just returned from northern Arizona where he was part of a crew which had the unenviable task of fighting forest fires when his manic state became acute. Chuck's "cycle" was such that in the summer he would become uncontrollably manic. Conversely, in the winter he experienced unbearable depression and no amount of any medication known to be in existence could curb his bi-polar symptoms. Chuck's sister had also been diagnosed with manic depression and had been often hospitalized.

Chuck had a ravenous appetite. After every meal the food trays were collected and placed in the specially designed cart for transportation back to the dietary department. This is when Chuck would rifle through the trays and devour every morsel of left over food. He simply couldn't control himself. One afternoon Chuck wept as he related to me how ashamed he was of his behavior on the airline flight from Arizona and how he had humiliated his mother.

"I just can't control myself." he whispered through his tears.

One of the other things about Chuck's behavior which I will eternally remember is that he never seemed to sleep and during his sleepless nights he would slip into Carolyn's room to have sexual relations with her. Eventually Carolyn was transferred to Richmond State Hospital but before she departed she quietly informed Chuck that she was pregnant. He held back tears as he watched be Carolyn escorted, in leather restraints, to the elevator.

On the fourth of July 1976, the 200th anniversary of our nation's founding, Chuck and I were standing together watching the fireworks in the distance through the heavily screened windows. Suddenly Chuck burst into tears. I asked him what was wrong and with tears running down his cheeks he said, "This is the fourth 4th of July in a row that I have spent up here." My heart sank. It grieved me that even one person would have to spend their summers restricted to a psychiatric ward. I nearly wept myself.

Not long after that I was alone in the day room during one late afternoon. I was staring out of the window, taking in the streetscape, when Sarah (the young girl mentioned earlier) came to me, stood on her tiptoes, wrapped her tiny arms around my neck and tried to kiss me. It took nearly all of my strength to push her away. She forcefully embraced me again, then looked me in the eyes and said. "I want you to screw me." I pushed her away again. "No Sarah…." I said as gently as I could, "You're much too young for that."

At that time a mental health worker entered, pried Sarah's arms from around me and led her from the room. That evening we all were disturbed by the unearthly sound of Sarah in a seclusion room wailing like a wounded animal. The next morning Sarah was gone.

The O.T. Lady

At about the mid point of my incarceration in Lutheran Hospital's psychiatric unit I was transferred from my private quarters into a large room which I shared with three other men. My idiocy had become somewhat under control, therefore I was stunned when one of the nursing staff approached me with some new type of medication. I informed her that I seemed to be doing fairly well and would be quite satisfied to maintain the status quo. The nurse then bristled up and demanded I take the medication, because it was "doctor's orders."

With much apprehension I swallowed the two capsules with water and went walking down the corridor toward the dayroom. Twenty or so minutes later I was sitting on one of the sofas there and thumbing through a magazine when an

Intense, unpleasant and indescribable feeling came over me. The best terminology I can use to express that sensation was a feeling of acute anxiety which manifested itself in my midsection and caused my innards to be forcefully pressed into my diaphragm. Even that depiction falls far short of the reality. I felt as though I wanted to break free and run head long into whatever place my feet could take me.

I had a seemingly overwhelming urge to dash at a full gallop to my room, but restrained myself and walked very fast. Reaching my room, I flopped on my bed, curled up in the fetal position, and lay there trying not to tremble. That offered me some relief, so I was there on my bed, curled up and fully clothed for several days. I did not eat and don't remember even going to the toilet. During that time I drifted in and out of a light sleep and fought my way through the most hideous nightmares imaginable. Several times, when I was close to regaining my awareness, the unquenchable anxiety again wrenched my abdominal organs and I would force myself back into oblivion in order to escape the suffering.

At some point I was aroused out of my misery long enough to find myself being jostled.

"Hey! *Hey*"

I wearily raised my head and looking to my right in annoyance, discerned that I was being disturbed by the Occupational Therapist whom I (with much derision) referred to as the O.T. lady.

"C'mon! You are going to O.T."

"Leave me *alone*!!" I roared.

The O.T. lady then took me by my arm and pulled me from the bed. Barely about to stand, much less walk, I was virtually dragged to the O.T. room where I was forced brusquely into a folding chair. I sat there slouching and staring holes in the O.T. lady as she began to speak.

"Today we are going to make mobiles."

"I don't want to make *mobiles!*" I snarled

"Mr. Holbrook, we *are* going to make mobiles!"

At that point I went off like a bottle rocket. I precariously got to my feet, let out with a string of words which would have caused 2 Live Crew to blush and staggered back to my room.

As I returned to my bed I found, on the bedside table, a brand new pair of eyeglasses. Evidently a local optometrist had fashioned them using the prescription from my old lenses. "What a thoughtful thing to do." I said to myself. Even though I was in absolute torment, I managed to crack half a smile.

Going Home

Other than the brief outing to the O.T. table, I had been in my bed for at least five days. On the fifth day (if my recollections are accurate), toward evening I was lying, in the fetal position, with my muscles agonizingly stiff, when I became aware of someone sitting near the foot my bed.

"Adam." A female voice said.

The voice had such an unmistakably gentle quality about it that I didn't seem to mind being disturbed. I opened my eyes and there sat a middle-aged nurse whom I had never seen before. The beauty which seemed to radiate from deep within her took my breath away.

I swung me feed off the bed and sat next to her, still doubled over.

"I know you have been having a hard time" The nurse said. "I have something here that will help you feel better."

"NO! *NO!*" I began to sob.

"No more medicine!! *Please!!* No more medicine!"

"You'll just have to trust me." The nurse replied.

After a few minutes of coaxing the nurse persuaded me to ingest the small white tablet. Within an hour I was up and walking around. I felt superb. What a release it was to at last feel "normal!"

The following week passed speedily and without incident. I was doing very well and received many words of encouragement from my fellow patients as well as the hospital staff. So much so that I garnered a unanimous vote from my group therapy partners (doctor included), who were vouching for my fitness to be discharged.

I was thrilled by the prospect of being released from the hospital after weeks of detention. It never dawned on me that I really didn't have anyplace to go. Rhonda and Glenn had moved into the house in Syracuse. Everything Cindy and I owned was now being stored in the garage there. Cindy had been staying with her parents all this time.

I will offer one more disgusting sidelight to my story. You will recall that as I left to pick up Cindy from the hospital in Warsaw I had locked our two dogs in the garage of our house in Syracuse. Well, when

Rhonda and Glenn, went to the house days later it reeked with a foul odor. As Glenn opened the garage door, he upchucked.

The garage floor was covered by a two inch layer of dog excrement. Both dogs also were caked with dung. Glenn vomited again as he immediately took Duke and Toby outside to be hosed off. The landlord was beside himself with rage when informed of condition in which Cindy and I had left the house.

Anyway, the hospital staff allowed me one call to make arrangements for my trip home after discharge. Cindy's parents had no telephone, but I did manage to get in touch with the next door neighbors. Within five minutes Cindy's mother came on the line. I asked if Cindy and I could stay temporarily in their home.

"Seeing as though you don't have anywhere….." a pause of twenty or so seconds…."I suppose it would be all right. Cindy Jean's dad will be over as soon as he gets off work." I thanked my mother-in-law liberally and with a smile on my face, hung up.

I spent the next two or so hours staring restlessly out of the window at the end of the short corridor from which I had an unobstructed view of the street below. I was fidgeting in my chair due to the fact that I was in a rush to get out of there. A nurse then come into view with some medication in one hand and what appeared to be a prescription in the other.

"You need to take this before you leave." She said with a devilish scowl. As I swallowed the medicine she gave me a malicious smirk, and then strode speedily away.

Within fifteen or so minutes I was overcome with the same excruciating sensation which had kept me in bed for several agonizing days. I didn't then have a bed to get into, so the only way to cope with my distress was to rock violently back and forth, as if I were in a rocking chair.

So I rocked….and rocked. I was still rocking when my father-in-law arrived to transport me back to Lima. Half of the way home, as I rocked, he looked at me and asked, rather coarsely, "Can you *stop* that?"

Home?

Upon arrival at my "home" John and I were treated to a high-spirited welcome by the family's three dogs who seemed to be the only ones who were delighted to see us. Cindy seemed indifferent, and Marilyn (my mother-in-law) was visibly annoyed, which did not at all surprise me.

As we sat down to dinner, I could almost smell the animosity which my in-laws felt toward me. After all, I had not been the ideal husband to their little girl. I was most willing to own up to that fact. As we dined in virtual silence, I made an altogether heroic effort to stifle the nearly maddening compulsion to rock in my chair. I did not succeed. Marilyn callously scolded me several times in her fear that I would ruin the wooden dining room chair on which I was sitting.

The effect of the medication was precisely the opposite of what everyone had hoped for. After dinner we had a discussion in the living room. It was decided that I would continue on the medicine for a few more days to ascertain whether or not the nasty side effects would subside. The four of us (literally) scraped together the funds to get the medication and John made an excursion to the nearest pharmacy.

For the following week all I could do to get relief from the severe attacks of nervousness which beleaguered me in every waking minute was to lie on a bed, rest the sole of my right foot on the mattress and violently swing my knee back and forth. I drove Cindy into a frenzy with this maneuver and on many nights deprived her of needed rest. She finally came to the point of insisting that I sleep on the living room floor.

It was during this week that Cindy's uncle Ralph came to visit. As we sat alone on the porch swing (with my right knee swaying from left to right) Ralph said he had come to speak with me. He then began to say that I was a man who now had a family and that I should be seeking some gainful form of employment. He was saying that I should come to understand that I had responsibilities. In the middle of that sentence I leaped to my feet, ran into the house and hurried directly to the bedroom. I assumed my "position" on the bed and then began to vigorously wave my right knee to and fro.

Uncle Ralph was livid. He shouted at me through the bedroom window that I was no good and could never amount to anything. He shouted that he was ashamed his niece could ever get hooked with up to a no account loser like me. I remained on the bed until after dark all while thinking that Uncle Ralph had been right. I never would be anything other than what I was, a "stinking pile of left over turds!." For the first time in weeks, I contemplated suicide.

Also in that week Cindy and I were invited by one of her school friends, Mark, to come and visit. Mark and his young wife, who was also pregnant, lived a few houses down the street. Mark and Jeanie were temporarily residing with his parents in order to get their marriage started on firm financial footing. They were terrific hosts and we decided that the four of us would play a game of Monopoly.

During the time of our visit I had, with much difficulty, controlled my spontaneous movements. But there came a moment in which I could no longer restrain myself. I suddenly jerked to my feet, spilling the tokens and play money all over the floor. I wanted to cry and nearly did before I dashed out of the door. Greatly embarrassed, Cindy apologized profusely and joined me outside. Furious, she slapped my shoulder several times as we walked "home." I buried my face in my hands wept all the way.

I was convinced that Mark probably never wanted to see me again. Therefore I was both astonished and gratified when he appeared at our door the next day and offered me a temporary job. Mark had been working for a local farmer and he said there was room for me on the crew of farmhands. I was delighted, and as graciously as I could, accepted. I realized that I would never get rich on this job, but hey, it would give me something with which to occupy myself plus provide a chance to earn an honest dollar.

Bright and early the next morning Mark came by to pick me up for work. As I stepped into the auto and closed the door I noticed that the radio was playing. I looked at it and winced. I was overcome by the fear of once again being drawn into the maelstrom of believing myself to be a Grammy award winning song writer. As I stared with intensity at the radio, Mark sensed that I was becoming uneasy.

"Does that bother you?" he asked with genuine concern.

"No! No!" I responded.

"I think I'll turn this off." Mark said as he switched off the radio. "I don't like that station anyway" Then he managed to give me a very sad smile.

False Labors

Toward the middle of August Cindy and I were invited to have Sunday dinner at the home of one of her distant cousins. A short while after dining sumptuously Cindy began to experience pain in her abdomen. Her female relatives (all of whom had given birth to several offspring) were convinced that the onset of Cindy's labor had come. They recommended that she walk because a stroll would help ease her into our baby's birth. We walked around the block several times and Cindy let me know she was tired and wanted to sit for a while. We returned to the house and as we entered, liquid began to flow from her lower abdomen, fully soaking her clothing.

Everyone (including me) was certain that Cindy's "water" had broken. After another hour or so of periodic pain, Cindy's cousins convinced me that I should drive her to the hospital.

After examining Cindy the attending physician informed us that labor had not started and the "water" was in fact urine. It seemed the baby had been laying on Cindy's urinary bladder.

Approximately a week earlier than that, after I could no longer tolerate the fierce urge to vigorously move as if seated in a rocking chair, I had discontinued taking the medication. The relief from the misery literally came within hours. I was at last able to sit still and relax normally. However, my mental instability again became manifest and within days after the previously mentioned dinner I was admitted to the psychiatric unit of St. Rita's Medical Center.

Early on the second day after my admission, a staff member informed me that Cindy had, late the night before, had been admitted to the same hospital due to complications related to her pregnancy. I was completely distraught after hearing this piece of bad news. After much pleading and cajoling the doctor grudgingly gave permission for me to visit Cindy unescorted for twenty minutes.

When I arrived in her room Cindy, looking pallid, reported that the doctor had just left and she would be allowed to go home later that day. After a short visit and a quick kiss and with tears in my eyes, I left Cindy and made my way back to the psychiatric floor. I was to be discharged three days later with a stern warning that I shouldn't allow myself to be caught in stressful circumstances.

"What a *JOKE*!!" I thought to myself. "Don't get stressed?!"

To get immediately to the point, (in order not to bore you, the reader with a lengthy dissertation) Cindy was to be once again admitted to St. Rita's Medical Center and this time she was not to return home without our baby.

August 23, 1976

I was awakened by the sound of someone energetically pounding on the front door. As I struggled out of the bed I glanced at my watch.

"6:15 am? Who's coming to the house at this hour?" I asked myself as I staggered down the hallway, making my way to the door.

By that time Cindy's parents, who had also been sleeping, were up and I nearly collided with Marilyn at the door. Outside was Cindy's cousin Jimmy.

"Adam!" he shouted. "The hospital called! You have to get there right now! They're taking Cindy Jean to surgery!"

I dashed back to the bedroom, jumped into my clothing and darted out the door without so much as combing my hair.

After arriving at the hospital I hurried to the maternity ward just as two nurses in surgical garb were moving Cindy out of her room. They informed me that a cesarean section was being performed because the baby couldn't pass through Cindy's narrow pelvis. Cindy was in painful labor and in a state of near panic. I had just enough time to squeeze her hand and run my hand over her golden locks. Then she was gone - wheeled down the corridor to the waiting staff in the operating room. I swallowed hard and made my way to the father's waiting room to find it empty. I was alone. It was the most momentous event since my wedding and I had to cope with it by myself.

After a few minutes I began to wonder what was taking so long. "Were there complications? Was the baby okay? Was Cindy okay?" I recalled being admonished to stay clear of stressful situations.

Yeah. Right.

After a span of time which I felt was entirely too long a nurse appeared at the door.

"Mr. Holbrook. You have a beautiful baby boy."

I was, to say the least, overwhelmed as a flood of indescribable emotions coursed through me.

"A son! I have a son!" I repeated to myself. I remained nearly incapable of grasping the enormity of the moment.

"I have a *son*!"

A few hours passed and when Cindy had recovered sufficiently from the anesthesia we were at last allowed to hold our son.

Cindy was glowing, as only a new mother could.

"Oh! He's adorable!"

I pulled the blanket from the face of my baby and exclaimed,

"He doesn't have any teeth!"

"He's not supposed to have teeth." Cindy said with a chuckle.

"I want to name him Daniel." I stated, still grinning from ear to ear.

"Daniel Adam." Cindy proclaimed.

It came to be my turn to hold Daniel and I ever so gently lifted him from the arms of his mother. I gazed into the little face of my newborn son - and shed tears of joy. Swiftly the remembrance of that horrific summer commenced to soften and fade, as if it had all been leading up to that glorious moment. That summer of

1976 was, it seemed, but a tumultuous prelude to the elation and peace which I felt at that moment.

Since August 23, 1976, my life has been further enriched by the birth of three additional blessings, Brian, Amanda and Kellie. Each in their own unique way, my four offspring never cease to bring me joy. I also now take pleasure in my two delightful grandchildren. Through them, I will live on.

October 9, 2014

Books by by Adam Holbrook

A tormented man, in this true story, reveals the tortures and trials of his life as a schizophrenic; a life lived on the streets and in shabby boarding houses; a life in which he might find himself in Chicago one day and in Denver another- far from his home in Lima, Ohio.. Anyone who has an interest in the struggles of the mentally ill will find this book both captivating and enlightening..
$9.95

In this sequel to Dear Mom, Adam Holbrook takes the reader on a fascinating first person journey into the sordid world of the mentally ill. On the pages of Shining On Adam relives for you his experiences while on the road to recovery from mental illness. Some are grisly, others are laughable and some may bring you to tears, but all are graphic, informative and entertaining.
$9.95

If you enjoy nostalgia, poetry, painful introspection and and homespun philosophy, you will enjoy The Bantam Rooster. From recollections of his upbringing in rural Ohio during the late fifties and early sixties, from heartfelt poetry and to letters written to five deceased friends, Adam captures the full spectrum of human emotion. In writing of this book, Adam discovered for himself what it truly means to be human in all its joys and also its heartbreaks. The Bantam Rooster is a touching journey not only into the soul of the author, but the reader's as well.
$9.95

All books 9.95
To Order See Adam Holbrook on
www.ebay.com or call 419.581.8576

Free Shipping

Printed in the United States
By Bookmasters